expect more

exceedingly abundantly
Ephesians 3:20

a daily tool for learning to expect and believe

by Rachel Lovingood

We live in a culture that is all about 'more'. More money, more clothes, more shoes, more pleasure, more, more, more. The interesting thing is how we as believers settle for much less than 'more' when it comes to our relationships with Jesus.

It's time to expect more spiritually! Whether you have known Christ for some time or are a new believer, this study is for you if you are ready to 'take it to another level'. I continue to be reminded and challenged that my expectations are powerful influencers and that God is so much more than I often recognize. Let's find out what life can be like when we allow the power of God to work in and through us.

My prayer for us as we walk through this study comes from Ephesians 3:16-21. Verse 20 says "Now to Him who is able to do exceedingly abundantly above all that we ask or think, according to the power that works in us".

Wow did you catch that?....our God is able to do exceedingly, abundantly more that we can even imagine....that is huge! and that is what we are trying to capture. May we be women who expect more from ourselves and from our God. Oh that He will blow our minds with who He is and who He wants to be in us.

I'm praying for you!
JOYfully,

Rachel

How to use "Expect MORE":

This study can be used as a quiet time/devotional guide or as a Bible Study for individuals or groups. The 15 days can be studied straight thru or divided into 3 weeks of 5 days.

The goal:
*provide you with a tool to help you begin living daily in the power that is available to you.
*Challenge and inspire your personal walk with Christ by studying different people who have 'expected more'
*help you identify what 'expecting more' looks like for you
*experience life change that happens when you 'expect MORE'

Each day or lesson has 2 sections. **Learn it!** includes Scripture references, devotional thoughts and study questions. **Live It!** is mostly thought provoking questions that challenge and equip you to apply the Truth of the Word to your daily life.

The expect MORE study has three main themes. First is to *expect* more. I've also been convicted that many of us as Christians must learn to *need* more Jesus and to *choose* more Jesus. You will see these three words as themes throughout the study-I hope they resonate with you as they have me.

MORE-the acrostic

Learn it!
I love memory tools. They really are effective for helping us grasp the meaning of the base word and to remember the different applications or meanings. That said, of course I want to start with an acrostic of MORE.

If we are going to grasp what it means to 'expect more' then we really need to know what it looks like for us personally. The concept of 'more' is a bit daunting and can really mean alot of different things. So let's take the word MORE and break is down into some doable pieces.

M is for Make Spiritual Growth a Priority
O is for Opportunity Taker
R is for Remember the Why
E is for Engage in the Battle

In what areas of your life have you been settling for less than 'more'?
marriage_____
parenting_____
work _____
personally_____
spiritually _____
other_____

Why do you think that you have allowed your expectations to be set low in these areas?

There are many reasons why we are tempted to set the bar low. It could be that you don't feel like you deserve any better because of guilt and shame over past mistakes. Or maybe you have never felt worthy of more because you have listened to the lies of the Enemy and even some people in your life. You may have low expectations because you never realized that there was another option.

Whatever the reason, let today be the last day that you think you are not a candidate for expecting MORE.

Look at the following verses and write what is true about you from each.

✱Psalm 139:13

✱Psalm 139:16

✱Ephesians 2:10

✱Jeremiah 29:11

Live It!
Those are a great start. Write at least one of these verses on something you will see daily. Whenever you are tempted to give up on expecting MORE, use it to remind yourself that God loves you enough to die for

you and that He has great plans for your life if you choose to let Him.

Write out a prayer asking God to show you where you have set the bar too low.

Now list what you plan to do to start making changes and raising the bar. For instance "I will take time to read the Word daily so that I can know Him better."

You're off to a great start! Stick with it, there is so much MORE to come.

"I pray that out of his glorious riches he may strengthen you with power through his Spirit in your inner being, so that Christ may dwell in your hearts through faith. And I pray that you, being rooted and established in love, may have power, together with all the saints, to grasp how wide and long and high and deep is the love of Christ, and to know this love that surpasses knowledge--that you may be filled to the measure of all the fullness of God. Now to him who is able to do immeasurably more than all we ask or imagine, according to his power that is at work within us, to him be glory in the church and in Christ Jesus throughout all generations, for ever and ever! Amen."

Ephesians 3:16-20

Underline the parts that speak to you the most from these verses.

Make Spiritual Growth a Priority

Learn it!
The M is where we start digging in to what expecting MORE really means for you personally.

What do you think it means to make growing spiritually a priority?

Read **2 Timothy 1:7-8**. What does it say about spiritual exercise?

Just as athletes need to practice the basics to get better at their games, Christ followers need to be involved in some spiritual basics or disciplines to grow stronger. Look at the partial list of disciplines below and whether you have ever seen them or not, take time to evaluate yourself on each one. Grade yourself from A-F.

➡Prayer
➡Bible Study
➡Worship
➡Evangelism
➡Fasting
➡Tithing/giving
➡Serving

Have you ever noticed that we tend to do the things that we like to do and avoid those that are uncomfortable for us? If you want to grow spiritually you have to be intentional and well balanced. But there is only so much time in a day and you are probably wondering where you can carve out a few minutes to focus on your spiritual growth. Be honest. You make time for what is important to you.

It helps to recognize what you refuse to compromise on. Let's call these the non-negotiables. Things like family time, sleep, etc.
List the non-negotiables in your life and how much time a day you spend on each.

Now list other major things you spend time on. Estimate how much time a day you spend on each.

What time is left? Hint: There are only 24 hours in a day so keep it real.

Live it!
Read Matthew 6:33. What does it say about your priorities?

How does this verse encourage you about making your spiritual growth first priority?

When you take time for the most important things it helps with your perspective on other things. What areas of your life do you need some perspective on because they are out of order?

Ask God for wisdom and strength to get your schedule lined up in a way that is pleasing to Him.

Be very careful, then, how you live--not as unwise but as wise, making the most of every opportunity, because the days are evil. Therefore do not be foolish, but understand what the Lord's will is.

Ephesians 5-15-17

Nothing is Impossible

Learn it!

Picture this. Teenage girl just visited by an angel and told that she has been chosen to be the mother of the Savior. She knows it isn't possible by human standards but in her response to the angel she reveals something very important about herself.

Read Luke 1:37 and write down what she said.

Mary was a strong believer. She had a faith like we need ourselves. How many times has the fact that you can't figure out how God could work something out kept you from obeying?

Maybe you felt convicted to start tithing or giving more money to the Lord but when you look at your bills you couldn't see how that would possibly work. Or you have heard about submitting to your husband but since he isn't as strong a Christian as you and has less convictions about spiritual things, you continue to stand up to him on every issue you can. Girlfriends-- nothing is impossible with God!!!

That's a great lesson from this teenager but how does that relate to 'Make spiritual growth a priority'? It's like this, Mary was raised in a traditional Jewish family so she was subjected to various religious teaching and instruction. She made it a priority even as a youngster and before you start thinking that there is no way we can know that for a fact, look at Luke 1:46-55.

After Mary got her startling and humbling news, she went to visit her relative Elizabeth. When Elizabeth confirmed the news of the angel, Mary broke out in to a song of praise that is quite famous called the Magnificat. During this song, Mary actually quotes numerous passages of Old Testament Scriptures. Look it up online or in your Bible and from the cross references, see how many different verses of OT Scriptures you can find referenced._____

That means that she knew her stuff. She hadn't been daydreaming when the priest read from the Scriptures or when her family talked about their religious heritage.

Mary had obviously made spiritual growth a priority and unknowingly she was preparing herself for the biggest responsibility in history--being the mother of Jesus.

Live it!
What opportunities do you regularly have to grow spiritually?

Would you say that you make the most of those times or that you take them for granted?

How can you see growing stronger spiritually affecting each of the following areas of your life positively?
*marriage

*family

*friends

*money

*work

*church

What is one thing that God has called you to, like Mary, but that you have resisted doing because you don't really understand how it could possibly work out?

Will you choose to step out in faith and say "with God all things are possible"? Tell Him you are willing.

Write out an "I am willing" prayer.

Opportunity Taker

Learn it!

Are you ever too busy for other people? Is your schedule so tight that you can't squeeze anyone or anything else in?

It's a common challenge for all of us in this busy culture and the Bible has some instructions that apply. Read Ephesians 5:15-16.

What are the 2 choices of how we can live?

Circle the one you want to be. What do the verses say to be careful about so that you can live wisely?

If you want to live carefully and wisely then what do you need to 'make the most of'?

_____

Some versions of the Bible translate this word as 'opportunity' or 'time'.

The original word in Greek is 'kairos', which is about more than just the minutes passing on the clock.[1] This word means both opportunity and time but with the added implication of 'God-ordained'. Wow! These are those moments in which God brings someone across your path at a specific time and place for a reason. There are no coincidences.

Here's the cool thing. There are 24 hours in a day which is 1440 minutes. That's it. It's all you get, no matter what the magazine covers promise you about 'adding hours to your days'. BUT by being intentional you can make the most of more 'kairos' moments and those are the ones that matter most.

When was the last time you experienced a 'kairos' moment?

A harder question to answer would be when was the last time you missed a God ordained moment? You've looked at how you spend your 1440 minutes daily, now let's talk about how to make the most of every opportunity.

The key goes back to the first of verse 15 which talks about choosing to live wisely. You may be wondering "How am I supposed to be wise?' Good question. Read James 1:5.

Where does wisdom come from? _____

How does God give wisdom? _____

So--if you want to live wisely then you need to ask God for wisdom and take time daily to seek Him. And according to James, you don't have to worry about any feelings of unworthiness because God gives 'without finding fault'.

Live it!
What does it mean to you that you don't have to be perfect to receive wisdom and be actively making the most of every opportunity?

Write out a prayer for wisdom and ask to be more sensitive to the opportunities that God brings you.

What are some 'kairios' opportunities you've had recently?

Keep your eyes open to the possibilities that are coming your way. That lady at the grocery who looks worn out--may need to know that someone cares. That neighbor who is feeling lonely may need to be invited to join the fellowship at your church. There are people all around that God has brought near you for a reason. Be aware and be intentional.

Prayer list of those who need to know Jesus

Name	Date I shared with them

A Divine Appointment

Learn it!

The story of Philip and the Ethiopian is a perfect picture of being an opportunity taker. There are some great tips we can learn from it to help us make the most of all our opportunities.

Read Acts 8:26-37.

How long did Philip wait to do what God told him to do?

Tip #1- Obey Immediately. Delayed obedience is disobedience. What is the danger you can see from waiting too long to respond to God?

Think about what would have happened if Philip had waited until he had gotten a new outfit for a road trip. He would have missed God's appointment for him and missed out on the blessing.

How did Philip start the conversation?

Tip #2 - Ask Questions. Break the ice with some questions. How are you today? What did you think about that sermon? Have you ever thought about_____? Is there anything I can pray for you about? These are just a few ideas to get started. Add any others you can think of.

What did Philip share with the man?

Tip #3- Go With What You Know. Talk about what you know or have experienced. You don't need to have all the answers. Just talk about Jesus and the way He has impacted you. Notice that when Philip saw what the man was reading, he recognized that as a good starting place.

How did the encounter end?

Tip #4- Offer the Opportunity to Choose. Give people an opportunity to commit to Christ or make changes.

Live It!
Which tip is the greatest challenge for you? Why?

How will you be more prepared to be an opportunity taker like Philip?

List the names of three or four people you have had divine encounters with recently.

Is there any way you can follow up on those conversations? Commit to doing so this week.

Remember the 'Why'

Learn it!
This is an important step in our quest to expecting MORE. If you haven't already noticed, you soon will, that knowing God better and seeking after Him is not always easy. The more you seek Him and surrender your life to Him, the more active your enemy gets.

How does 1 Peter 5:8 describe your enemy?

What is the advice to you for protection?

Sometimes it seems the more we focus on Christ, the harder our lives become. That's because Satan wants you to give up and settle for ho hum kind of faith. Once you choose Jesus, your eternity is set and Satan can't get your soul. He then changes his focus to preventing you from being an effective witness for the Lord. If he can get you distracted by tough circumstances and cause you to doubt your faith then he wins that battle and you settle into a powerless kind of life.

When the going gets tough, the wise believer focuses on why it all matters anyway.

Read Romans 10:13-14. What happens to those who call on the name of the Lord?

Hallelujah! We are saved and will spend eternity in heaven. But what happens to those who haven't called on the Lord? Where do they spend eternity? _____ Right, in a very real place called Hell.

Notice what verse 14 says our responsibility is. We must be active in telling others and sharing our faith. FYI the word in verse 14 'preached' doesn't have to be by a pastor or preacher but it actually means "to proclaim openly something which has been done".[2]

That very simply means that if you have trusted in Jesus, then it is your responsibility to tell openly what has happened to you. You have been rescued from eternity in Hell and been given Heaven. That is a huge deal and that is what 'remembering the why' is all about.

Live It!
What circumstances have been distracting you from telling people about your faith or talking about Jesus?

How can remembering the 'why' encourage you to live differently and persevere through tough stuff?

When you think about lost people dying without Jesus and going to Hell, who are you most worried about?

Pray for each of these people by name and then ask God to give you the perfect 'kairos' moments to talk to them about Jesus. You don't have to preach a beautiful sermon, just tell them who Christ is to you and what He is doing in your life.

Answer the questions below to help organize your thoughts and prepare you to talk about what Jesus has done in your life.

What was I like before being saved?

What made me realize I needed a Savior?

What is my life like now? (How am I different?)

It really is that simple. You can't get it wrong because it's your life and your relationship. Be honest and be real. Remember the 'why' and speak boldly because reality for those who die without Christ is Hell. That should be strong enough to get us talking and help us push through the difficulties that come our way.

Find People to Share With: Use this simple diagram to identify people in your current spheres of influence that you may have the opportunity to share with. Write your name in the center circle. Use the spokes to identify places you routinely go and write names of people you encounter at each on lines off the spokes of those who may be lost. Pray over this list and be ready!

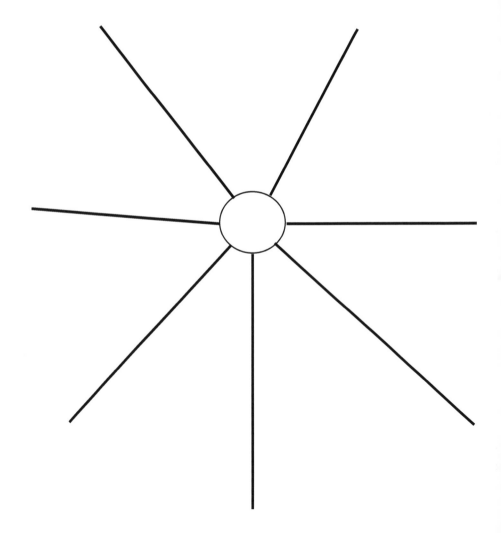

Engage in the Battle

Learn it!
As you change and become more and more like
Jesus you may notice more conflict. Read 1 Peter
2:11 and James 4:1 to identify some of the sources of
conflict. List them here:

Although there are these battles within us, there is
also a very real war playing out around us. What does
Ephesians 6:12 say our battle or struggle is against?

This is all about the war between good and evil, light
and dark and we have a job to do.The person that
expects MORE is also unwilling to sit back and let
darkness take over. It is our right and privilege to do
all we can to push back darkness and advance the
kingdom of God.

The different kinds of battles are connected. Every
time you resist giving in to your sinful nature, you
strengthen your faith and that pushes back at
darkness. Every time you submit to God and follow
His plan to share your faith, you push back darkness.

What are sone other examples you can think of that
push back darkness?

It can be intimidating to think of yourself in this way but here's a cool thought. You can only engage in the battle successfully when you do it the way that God describes in His Word.

Read Ephesians 6:14-17.

What are some pieces of the armor of God that you are told to put on?

girded with _____
breastplate of _____
feet shod with _____
shield of _____
helmet of _____
sword of the _____

According to verse 14 if you put on this armor of God what will you be able to do when the battle comes your way?

It's comforting to realize that you don't have to stand against the schemes of the enemy on your own power and strength.

Live It!
Which of the following best describes you in regard to engaging in the battle? Why?

draft dodger
MIA (missing in action)

dedicated soldier
POW (prisoner of war)
front line fighter
walking wounded
other _____

Are you pleased with your choice? Put a star by the
one that you wish described you.

What will it take for you to become who you want to
be in this battle between good and evil? (list at least 3
specific things)

1.

2.

3.

There are so many people who have given us great
examples of standing strong for the faith. In the next
days you will have the opportunity to study individuals
from the Word and gain some good insights into how
you can expect MORE daily.

Thank God for specific people you can think of who
have engaged in the battle. Write their names here
and if they are still living, take time to thank them for
their example of courage.

Notes:

An Unlikely Soldier of Faith

Learn it!
There are many things that can hold us back from being engaged in the battle. Fear, past mistakes, feeling unworthy, lack of knowledge--any of these and many more can be keeping us from MORE living.

Please read with fresh eyes a great story of a woman who had every reason to stay on the sidelines and let everyone else fight the battle. Yet she didn't let anything stop her from being a major player in God's story. Read Joshua 2:1-11.

Who is our heroine?
What was her profession?

Well, that's a couple of strikes against her. A woman, with a bad past. How in the world could God use someone like that to achieve one of the greatest victories for His people? It's because of what she said about the Lord. She recognized Him for who He was and she believed in what she had heard about Him.

This was taking place during the time when the children of Israel, under Joshua's leadership were preparing to go into the Promised Land and take possession. The problem was that there were already people living there and they had been hearing about the huge group of people with the different 'God' moving in their direction. Anyone else who wanted to believe in the Lord could have, but it seems that

Rahab was the one who stood out and risked everything to help the spies.

We've already established that the battle is here. Like Rahab, we have to ask ourselves if we are willing to do what it takes to help the Lord's army win.

Live It!
What are some things that you have let hold you back from engaging in the battle for the Lord?

What strikes you from Rahab's story that encourages you to step out?

Rahab went on to be a woman of great faith (she left her former profession) and is actually listed in the genealogy of Christ. All because she made the right choice to trust in God and follow Him in the middle of difficult circumstances.

What circumstances do you need to trust God in today so that when you look back you can know that you laid it all on the line? Remember-it is impossible for God to let you down.

The Issue of Need

Learn it!

This is a good time to address some of the obstacles we face in our quest to expect MORE. Many of us are similar to a familiar character in Scripture. Read Matthew 19:16-26.

This is the story of the rich young ruler. Before you skip over it thinking that it doesn't apply to you, understand that the term 'rich' means abounding in material things. That's all of us. If you live in the United States then you most likely live above the poverty level of the rest of the world. You are 'rich' so take a minute to see what you can learn and apply from this passage.

What does Jesus tell the young man to do in order to receive eternal life?

What is the man's response?

Notice that Jesus said it is hard for a rich man to enter the kingdom of heaven. But later in verse 26, how does Jesus say it is possible?

The more we have, the less we need Him, we have it all. Please don't miss this. So many times in our lives we miss out on expecting MORE and experiencing MORE with Jesus because we just don't *need* Him.

Wow, that was a tough statement but how true do you see it in your life?

Can I suggest that when we recognize our great need for Him daily then we will start expecting MORE daily? You and I often fall into the trap of our own comfort zones. We begin to feel like we have it all together and can handle life. The reality is that we need Jesus. Today, tomorrow and every day if we want to really live exceedingly and abundantly beyond our imagination.

Read Exodus 16:4. As it describes the provision of God for the children of Israel, how often are they told to gather what they need?

What is the reason for it being a daily activity?

The Lord knew that humans have a tendency to run their own lives and rely on their own strength so He made sure that they would learn to trust Him for even their basic need for food--daily.

Check out the example that Jesus gave as He taught His followers to pray. What does Luke 11:3 say to pray for?

How often?

The word translated for daily bread there means "bread of our necessity".[3] Or think of it as 'what we need to live'. We cannot get past the fact that we are our strongest spiritually when we are relying and trusting in Him for our daily provisions.

Live It!
What are some signs that you have so much you don't need Jesus?

What are the things or people that you tend to count on instead of Jesus?

Make it a habit this week to begin your day by declaring your dependence on God. Tell Him how much you need Him and ask for the daily provisions only He can give.

When you notice that you are thinking you have it all together or that you can handle life on your own, stop and confess that to God. Then be intentional about changing your mindset immediately to one of gratitude for His leadership.

*Recognize that He supplies all our needs. If your wants are out of control then that is something else to address.

In what specific areas of your life are you guilty of excess?

My Very Own Lord's Prayer
Use the model prayer in Luke 11 and write out
your own Lord's prayer. Personalize it according
to your life and use first person.

When all Else Fails

Learn it!

How about a look at someone who recognized his need for God after all else he could have relied on was gone? Moses was an Israelite who grew up in Pharaoh's palace with all the privileges that came with his adopted family. He had access to many things that his people did not. If anyone was prepared to be a leader of great success who could handle life on his own, it would have been Moses.

Then something interesting happened. Moses lost his position in Pharaoh's household because he stood up for one of his countrymen and he had to run for his life. He spent the next 40 or so years in the desert as a shepherd (not exactly a prestigious position).

Read Exodus 3:1-5. What got Moses's attention?

Who was speaking to him and why?

In Exodus 4:1-9 you can read about the miracles that God displayed to encourage and strengthen Moses' faith.

Read Exodus 4:10. What words would you use to describe Moses' state of mind?

Notice that this fear and uncertainty were expressed just after being the sole witness to some pretty cool miracles including being spoken to by the Lord from a bush that was burning but not burning up!

After all his years in the desert, out of the spotlight of Egypt, Moses' response to God's call was something like "Are you sure you have the right guy?" "You do know that I stutter and don't talk so good?" Isn't it funny that although we know that God knows what He is doing, when He calls us, sometimes all we can focus on are our weaknesses?

What are some weaknesses you have that you think might limit how God can use you?

Understand that Moses' 40 years in Pharaoh's house then his 40 years in the desert were not wasted. God was preparing Moses every step of the way to be the deliverer of His people. Imagine what kinds of skills Moses was developing as he herded sheep.

You my be able to relate to Moses' desert experience because you have been in one of those yourself. What are some things you learned or skills you developed during your desert time?

If you are currently in a desert period, start praying that God will continue to teach you things and prepare you for the next phase He has planned and then be sensitive to His voice when He speaks.

Live It!
Be honest. When was the last time you resisted obeying God because you felt your weaknesses were too much to overcome?

How does Moses' story challenge that kind of thinking and motivate you to rely on Him instead of your own self?

Be aware of another reality. Moses did move ahead in obedience but he continued to be plagued by his insecurities (they aren't just a woman thing) In Exodus 6:30. Moses gave God the same argument again.

How does it make you feel to realize that you aren't the only one who deals with insecurities?

What will you do the next time a thought of your inabilities or insecurities tempts you to refrain from following God in obedience?

Use Me Lord!

Gifts & Abilities	How God might want to use it.

Who's the Boss?

Learn it!

Have you ever thought about how many choices you make every day? Guess. It's probably even more than that. And there are many choices that we make without even being aware that we made them, but as a Christ follower there is one choice that you must be intentional about every day. Who's the boss?

Just as a car must have a driver, your life must have someone in control of it. There are only 2 options: yourself or the Holy Spirit. You choose.

The interesting thing about this control issue is that it must be made daily. Read Joshua 24:14-15.

This is a crucial time in the life of God's people. They have followed Joshua's leadership and been successful in taking the land. But there is danger in success and good times--it is these times in which we forget how much we need God and we begin to rely on other things or other 'gods'. Joshua is renewing the covenant that the Lord had made with this people many years before.

You may have heard the words of verse 15 before or seen it in a wall hanging, but did you ever realize what came just before it? Look back at chapter 24:1-13.

What does that sound like to you?

It sounds like a recap of God's activity in the lives of the people. Hmmm. Joshua was a brilliant leader who stopped to remind the children of Israel all that God had done on their behalf. THEN he challenged them to choose who they were going to serve.

Think about that lesson for us. We need to keep track of all that God is doing in our lives and replay it from time to time.

What are some benefits you can think of to replaying God's activity in your life?

Notice in verse 14 that Joshua gave three instructions. What are they?
1. fear the _____
2. serve God with _____ and _____
3. put away _____ _____

These are all good advice to help us in the choice of who is in control. The first two help us remember who He really is and who we are in relation. Now, focus in on number 3. The people had been in the habit of turning to other gods periodically. (A god is anything that we serve other than the Lord.) Joshua was pretty bold about the time to make the choice. When did he say in verse 15 that they needed to choose?

When is 'this' day? Right. It's always today. I love that! It means that we need to choose this day, right now, who we will serve-the god of ourselves or God?

Live It!
What other 'gods' are you most tempted to serve?
(self, kids, fame, power, money, happiness, image...)

What are some of the big things that you can recall
when you think through God's activity in your life?

How does remembering these things motivate you to
choose wisely on the issue of control?

Start each day with a confession of your relationship
with the Lord. Praise Him for being your Savior and
Lord then surrender your will to His today. Choose
'this' day to serve Him and live for Him. (You may
want to paraphrase Josh 24:15) Choosing MORE is
about choosing to give Him control.

My Spiritual Markers: Make a spiritual map of your life from as far back as you can remember. List the high and low points as you track God's hand.

12

Expecting MORE

Learn it!
There are literally hundreds of people in Scripture that
we can look at for examples of expecting MORE. One
is Elijah and his experience with the prophets of Baal
on Mt. Carmel. Read 1 Kings 18:21-39.

What does verse 21 challenge the people to do?

Exactly. Here it is again. The challenge to choose
between the gods of the world and the one true God.

What happened when the prophets of Baal tried to get
a response from their god?

What did Elijah do to the ox on his altar?

Why do you think he soaked the offering with water?

Reread verses 38-39.
What did God do to the offering?

How did the people respond?

He is a great example of expecting MORE. Elijah poured so much water on the altar that there could be no possibility of anyone or anything other than God burning it up with fire. He had that kind of confidence in the Lord. He also wanted to be sure that the credit for what was about to happen couldn't be given anywhere but where it belonged--on God.

That story makes no sense, unless you know God. If we live our lives of faith and expect only what we can understand from God then we are limiting His power in our lives. We can never expect more from God then He has the power or ability to do.

Live It!

How have you limited His activity in your life because you can't always understand it?

What situation in your life do you need to see God work in?

What can you gain and apply from Elijah's story that helps you to expect MORE?

13

Open My Eyes

Learn it!
Today is about us realizing who's team we are on and how much more powerful those that are for us are than those that are against us.

Elisha was a man of God, a prophet. At one time an opposing king was very frustrated because Elisha kept knowing what he was planning and disrupted all his plans. The only way that Elisha could possibly know these things was because God revealed them.

The King of Aram decided to do something about Elisha so he sent his troops to surround Dothan where Elisha was staying. Pick up the story at 2 Kings 6:14-19.

Why was Elisha's servant afraid?

He saw the overwhelming odds against them and reacted in fear.

How did Elisha instruct him to respond to the fear?

How many times is prayer your first response to fear? Or do you try everything else before you remember to pray? If we can learn to pray first, it will save us alot of heartache and stress.

Elisha's prayer revealed much about his faith in God. What does it say to you?

What is the reason Elisha gave to not fear?

How did he know that 'those with them were more than those against them'?

What did the servant see when his eyes were opened by the Lord?

Very cool. Do you ever wish to peel back the layers and be able to see inside the spiritual realm? It might shock us but I bet for sure it would motivate us to live right and choose God.

Live It!
The servant was distracted by what he saw that caused fear. What is distracting you today?

Use the following steps to walk through refocusing and avoiding distractions spiritually.
1. Stop the wrong thinking.
2. Confess it as sin.
3. Replace those thoughts with Truth (Scripture)
4. Ask God for strength to change and trust Him.

Don't be afraid to ask Him to open your eyes to see what you need to in order to walk by faith.

Living on E or F?

14

Learn it!

Have you ever tried to drive your car with the gas gauge on E? It's not the smartest thing to do. You won't get very far because it is extremely important what you put into your tank. The same is also true of us spiritually.

Read Romans 15:13.
What can we be full of?

How does this filling take place?

What is the power by which we can be filled with these good things?

You see, in order to live our lives the way that God desires us to, we need to be full of things that come through His Holy Spirit--in short, we need to be full of HIm. The cool thing is that He supplies us with the necessary power to accomplish this.

The word for 'full' used here is the same word used in Ephesians 3:19 and it means "filled to the brim" and implies being completely full even to the point of overflow. Imagine that. Being so full of hope by the Holy Spirit that you overflow it to those around you.

Live it!
Do the people you come in contact with get splashed with your joy and hope or something else??? What do you most often feel full of? Circle all that apply.

fear   grace   joy   love
hope   peace   stress   anger
   uncertainty   worry   patience

You probably circled a few things that you would rather not have. It's possible that you have been getting full of some things that aren't what God wants for you.

Look at the negative things you circled above and list them each below with their opposite spiritual characteristic.

The next step to making changes about what you are full of is to pray off the negative traits and pray on the spiritual opposite. Do that and you will begin to see changes occur.

One of the most effective ways to see these types of changes is to pray using Scripture. Look up the characteristics you want to see in your life and find a verse that you like, then pray that verse for yourself over and over.

There is power in praying the word of God. Use it!!

Possible Verses to Pray
Use these or list your own

Love----------John 15:12
Obedience------------Deut 11:27
Patience------------Hebrews 10:36
Self-control------------Galatians 5:22-23
Pure speech----------Prov 15:4
Pure thoughts-------------Phil 4:8
Wholeheartedness-------------Col 3:23
Discipline---------------- 1 Cor 9:27

15

Beware of Opposition

Learn it!

Congratulations! You've been diligent and focused on knowing God better and expecting MORE. That means that you need to be prepared for opposition to come.

In Acts chapter 3 the believers had been enjoying a time of great miracles and wonderful happenings...then chapter 4. Read Acts 4:1-14.

When did the opposition come on them?

Notice that the leaders of the persecution were the same men who had a hand in the sentencing of Jesus (that doesn't bode well for the good guys) What was the question they asked in verse 7?

The word used for 'power' here is the same word used when talking about the power that raised Jesus from the dead and the power we can live in as believers--it's the 'dunamis' power of God.[4]

It really doesn't get more powerful than raising from the dead! What a great question to be asked because it just opened the door for Peter to share the Gospel, which he did.

I love what verse 13 says. What did the rulers and elders notice about Peter and John?
They were just really plain, ordinary men who weren't all that special. Sound familiar? Aren't we all just ordinary people? Jesus was glorified in and through their lives because they followed Him and obeyed. They chose to live in the power of the Holy Spirit and it showed. We have the same option.

Live It!
Instead of feeling useless because you are ordinary, what can you take away from this story?

Opposition came suddenly but instead of freaking out, Peter and John had the opportunity to share the Gospel publicly. When opposition comes your way, are you prepared to resist the temptation to compromise by standing for Jesus?

Simple steps to prepare you for opposition:
Be convinced about the following:
1. Know what you believe about the BIble, Jesus, God, salvation and eternity.
2. How you will live. Your actions should back up your words. be a doer of the Word not just a hearer.
3. Who you obey. Are you listening to the Word or the world?

Use the next page to write out your statements of faith or Truths that you refuse to compromise on. (For example: I am convinced that Jesus is the son of God.)

I am Convinced that:

Thank you so much for investing in this journey with me. Let me know if you have thoughts or questions by emailing me rachel@rachellovingood.com or stop by my blog and leave a comment at www.rachellovingood.wordpress.com

You can also find me on twitter and facebook:)

Blessing to you as you expect MORE!!!!

[1] http://www.blueletterbible.org/lang/lexicon/lexicon.cfm?
Strongs=G2540&t=KJV

[2] http://www.blueletterbible.org/lang/lexicon/lexicon.cfm?
Strongs=G2784&t=NASB

[3] http://www.blueletterbible.org/lang/lexicon/lexicon.cfm?
Strongs=G1967&t=NASB

[4] http://www.blueletterbible.org/lang/lexicon/lexicon.cfm?
Strongs=G1411&t=NASB

Made in the USA
Columbia, SC
03 October 2021